Winter

Toronto, Ontario

Northwest Territories

Winter

Text by Morley Callaghan
Photographs by John de Visser

New York Graphic Society
Boston

International Standard Book Number 0-8212-0642-7
Library of Congress Catalog Card Number 74-14744
Published in Canada by McClelland and Stewart Limited
Published in the U.S.A. by New York Graphic Society Ltd.,
Boston

The Laurentians, Quebec

New Brunswick

Late one night I was at the front window of my Toronto home. It snowed. For hours it had been snowing, the first heavy fall coming in the middle of December. Heavy flakes drifting across the overhanging corner street light masked the familiar fences and trees. Beside me, his paws up on the window sill while he waited to go out on his run to the corner, was our big white standard poodle, who kept turning his head to me as if he couldn't figure out what was happening to his territory. He was a pup, just six months old. He had never seen snow. But for me it was the beginning of another white winter.

If you said tell me about the winters, I'd say what do I know about the winter, I have seen too many of them, they have been with me too long, they are part of my life, I can't separate myself from them, nor would I want to. Though I have said cynically many times that this country was founded on the glowing big-bellied stove and should have on the national flag not the maple leaf but the Quebec heater, and though some of my neighbors now will be preparing for the annual escape to the Bahamas, I am here where I was born, getting some kind of quiet pleasure watching the city get snowed in on this mild winter night. I always feel younger on such a night, especially if the moon comes out after it stops snowing.

My father used to smile and say that Kipling had called Canada Our Lady of the Snows, and the smile was like a wink, warning me that Kipling knew nothing about Canada. But a little Canadian kid doesn't know that there are strange lands where there is no snow. When you are very young you love the winter. A child comes along the street crying and shivering, his wet-mitted hands lifeless at his sides, his neck red from his wet scarf, and his feet soaking wet. But as soon as he gets home and has his mitts placed on the hot radiator, and his socks changed and pants dried, he rushes out again. As soon as he learns to walk he is given a sleigh for Christmas, or a toboggan and taken to some hill in a park. If his father says he is too young for skis he makes them out of barrel staves with strips of leather nailed

on them as hooks for your feet, and even before he can skate he is playing hockey
on the street, or on a hose-frozen rink in his backyard. And if, as he grows older,
he hears some teacher refer to the winter as "the great Canadian challenge", he
thinks the man is crazy.

Kids use the winter. They play with it. Winter happiness in Canada seems to
come to those who know how to use this season. Some even use it in a weird way,
for a satisfaction they can't get at any other time of year.

On our street when I was a kid a man of sixty-five lived alone in a house across
the street from us. In the summer months we hardly saw him. He didn't talk to his
neighbors. This woman, a widow, who lived to the left of him, said he was rather
surly in his aloofness and she no longer tried to speak to him. He was a tall, stooped,
thin man with a drooping gray moustache. When winter came and the snow fell this
isolated man would come out late at night with his shovel and slowly clear the
sidewalk, and then he would stand, leaning on his shovel looking up the street. It
didn't matter how deep and heavy the snow was. One night, after he had finished
shovelling his own snow, he shovelled the snow of the widow, his neighbor to the
left. In the morning the widow came across the street and talked to my mother. She
was distressed. She didn't know what to say to the man; if she thanked him he might
do it again, and how could she be sure what he was aiming at. She decided to ignore
him. When it snowed again he shovelled her walk again, and he kept on. Then, two
weeks later, he began to shovel the snow of the neighbor to the right of him, and
this woman had a husband. Now the old man had two upset neighbors who would
like to have said, "Please stop shovelling my snow," but they didn't like to speak
to him. He had always ignored them. All winter long he went on with his shovelling,
always late at night, and when he had finished the three places he would stand
leaning contentedly on his shovel.

We called him the snow man. This man certainly had learned how to use the

Saskatchewan

Toronto, Ontario

winter for some special personal satisfaction, whatever it was. Maybe it has been the same with me. What is it? It can't come from winter play, the hunting, the ice fishing, the skiing, the snowmobiling. Is it an inner satisfaction never to be quite named? Or it could be a liking for the country's dramatically violent contrasts in climate? Violent summers! Violent winters! After the summer maybe there is some kind of solace for the spirit in the snow and ice. Whatever it is, it gives a man good memories, and he often realizes this when he is in Europe and finds he gets irritated explaining that his country isn't all ice and snow in a long winter night.

One night years ago we were in Paris sitting at our Montparnasse cafe. An American friend came over to us. He had a pale, slender, sad-eyed, black-haired young Frenchman with him. He introduced him. The Frenchman was a poet. He had heard we were from Canada and he wanted to tell us his story. His lovely girl, to whom he had given everything, had run off with another man, a fellow of no talent, a bum devoid of sensibility, and now he was hurt and despairing and sick of his Parisian life. He had thought of suicide, he said with a wan smile. But that would be cowardly. Instead, he wanted to change his life, hurl himself into a wilderness of ice and snow. Canada was the place. He had read about Canada. He would become a trapper. Could we tell him what furs he could sell? There were otters and beavers and moose and deer and the lynx, weren't there? But above all what he wanted to know was what kind of sturdy clothes he should have.

"Always remember that in Canada the weasel in winter becomes a white ermine," I began, feeling irritated. Then I blurted out, "Look, you are worrying about the wrong thing. You should be concerned with how little clothing you will be able to wear so much of the summertime in Canada. And the black-flies in the steamy bush. It's hot there. Ice and snow are easy to handle. The heat, the awful summer heat is the thing. In the bush you pray for a wind to blow away the black-flies. In the cities you have to head for a lake. You'll find out what a relief it is when the winter comes and you can put on some clothes."

The young French poet stared at me in astonishment. "Is this true?" he asked. "It is very true about the summer," I said. When he had left, making it plain he was having second thoughts about burying his talents in the ice and snow of Canada, I turned on my American friend. "This is an old story with you Americans," I said, shrugging. "All you know about Canada you get from reading those ballads of Robert W. Service. Yukon ballads. *Look at my eyes, I've been snow blind twice,*" I quoted mockingly. *"Look at my foot, half gone,* or *Out of the night which was fifty below and into the din and glare* . . . . Come on, man, why don't you take a look at the map? *See where Canada is.*"

If he would really take a look and follow that borderline between Canada and the United States, I said, he would see that the southern tip of Ontario is farther south than the northern tip of California. And Detroit is just across the river from Windsor, and the climate of my own big city, Toronto, is about the same as the Boston climate. So why hadn't he told his despairing French poet to go bag a beaver in Boston? Or to go out to Minnesota, instead of Saskatchewan? What's the difference in climate, out there?

The bleak Arctic view of Canada seems to be set in the European mind and you can't do much about it. It was set a long time ago by those seventeenth-century French chroniclers who visited the early settlements along the St. Lawrence. I'm sure the young French poet had read them. Those journals are so grim they make you wonder why the French were bent on settling here. Or could it be that those chroniclers couldn't understand how men could handle such a winter? They tell of people dressed like bears, groping their way through deep snowdrifts. It was so cold that even the bears buried themselves for the winter. Settlers were found frozen stiff in snow banks. Men often had frozen arms or legs chopped off. A cruel, savage, icebound land. But why then did Champlain love the new world along the great St.

British Columbia

nine in the evening and twenty below zero. We were on our way to visit a professor friend. We couldn't get a taxi. We decided to walk, it was only ten blocks to the professor's house. There was a bitter wind. I was wearing my city overcoat, and it was no protection against the heavy, icy wind. We stopped at a crossing and I thought we were having an animated beautiful intellectual discussion about whether England's future lay in an acceptance that it was simply part of Europe. I began to shiver. The wind tore into my bones. My jaw began to tremble. I felt dizzy. Our voices, the discussion about Europe, sounded idiotic. Voices from a faraway, fantastic, warm other world. Then I really believed in those stories of the Winnipeg winters of '36 and '37, when it had been fifty below for days. Those winters seemed to be all around me slowly killing me as they had killed others who had wandered away from home. They tried to hide in snowbanks. Outside the city, cows and dogs had stood stiff and dead-bizarre monuments. All across the prairies, farmers had huddled around stoves, praying only that the fuel would last. They had used cow dung for fuel. Now I felt a numbness in me as I stood there holding the arm of my friend. It was the wind. I asked myself, what am I doing here? Is all of Canada a longing for Spring? "Faster, for God's sake, let's walk faster," I said to my friend. While the wind chewed away my face I seemed to have a profound insight into the growth of the astonishing Indian civilizations that had developed in Mexico and Peru. It had been a simple matter. Thousands of years ago Indians had come across the Bering Straits, moving south. The smart Indian, tasting this prairie winter, kept moving very fast. He kept running all the way to Mexico. The placid, slow-moving, dull Indians were left behind in what is now called Canada, where I was too, in the center of all the cold in the world. Why? Then we came to the house of our friend and into the incredible warmth, and the relief I felt made me tremble.

Well, my cold night in Winnipeg was admittedly a shameful experience-for a Canadian. I wasn't myself. I was caught offguard by the bitter heavy wind. It must

Ontario

Quebec City, Quebec

have weakened the spirit. It made me, for the moment, give in when I knew that the wonder of the country was that people never gave in to the winter. And anyway, the truth is that those western cities, Winnipeg, Regina, Calgary, Edmonton, seen in the fantastic winter sunlight, have a lovely sparkle. That's what should be remembered. Why, in Regina, come to think of it, it often didn't seem to be cold at all. It's the dry air, so crisp and exhilarating. One night when it was twenty-five below zero I was walking along blithely with a friend, feeling light and lively, with the northern lights swinging overhead as if a giant ribbon counter had been caught in an electric fan. When we passed under a street light my western friend said casually, "You better watch that ear. I think it's turning white." Hands over my ears, I headed for the nearest restaurant.

I think of that frost-bitten ear now, seeing it in my mind against the prairie wheat fields just before harvest time when you are looking across flat land for miles and miles from some high office building or hotel room, and this land with its ripening wheat is one big warm golden bowl in the sunlight. The contrast! The frozen ear, the warm glowing bowl. It's Canada. And just a few months later this golden carpet, when winter settles in, becomes an endless howling winter desert and those unpainted farm houses look bleak, cold and lonely against the wild winter extravagance of the northern lights. Then a sense of isolation literally reaches through the train window at you. It's winter loneliness. It's not like the summer prairie loneliness that has a touch of pleasurable melancholy to it when the moon rises and a dog barks and the land and the sky seem to come closer together in stillness, and evenness: no grandeur, nothing wild. Nothing wild? It is something of a prairie winter wildness that I always remember.

One February afternoon on a train crossing the prairies in a blizzard, the man who was sitting across from me, a westerner, friendly and loquacious, banged my knee. "Look, there they are," he said, "What did I tell you?" and I looked out.

The blizzard snow, coming in whirling patches, made a shifting cold gray screen against the window; then would come sudden clear patches that seemed to have endless depths till they too were screened. The man had been telling me that wild horses still roamed the prairie. I had never quite believed in these horses. But there, now, out there in the blizzard about a quarter of a mile away a herd of horses came charging along. Sometimes screened off, they became part of the blizzard. Sometimes they came into one of the clear patches as they raced along, ghost horses, tossing their heads, all white in the swirling snow, and I watched them raptly as if I suspected they were trying to tell me something with their ghostly dance.

Just the other day, here at home, I thought of those wild horses when a neighbor of mine who lives just up the street told me he had sold his house and was going west to Calgary. West in the winter time? Him? A young successful businessman here in the east? What was the magic? The wild horses? I kidded him. He missed the prairies, he said, and he missed especially the country around Calgary. And as for it being cold, hadn't I been there in the winter at the time of the warm Chinook winds. And hunting there was so close at hand; not a big expedition as it was here in the east. And anyway, the big action now in Canada was in the Alberta oil fields. Winter or summer, what was the importance of the weather when the action was all out there. "Well, I suppose, that seems to be a Canadian winter story; it never seems to be cold where the action is. Or maybe you go a little crazy out there wanting to watch some winter action, and maybe that's why they turn out to watch football in the end of the season, thousands of men, women and children, sitting in open stands, the thermometer hovering around zero, with the ball floating around in the falling snow. The west? No, the truth is they have done the same thing here in Toronto. I remember one Grey Cup time in Toronto when the temperature had dropped to seven above zero the night before the game. That night I was in a hotel with the out-of-town sportswriters who had come to cover the national event.

Erindale, Ontario

Toronto, Ontario

About midnight a veteran came in to the room where we were drinking. He had just walked a few blocks from a nearby restaurant. Wild-eyed and bitter, he took a drink and started cursing. "What am I doing covering a football game played on a rock-hard icy field with great banks of snow on the sidelines and the temperature dropping to zero? They call this sport, eh? We're all crazy. What am I proving with my teeth chattering? This is all wrong for football. If the temperature doesn't jump twenty degrees tomorrow, I won't cover the damn game." But by noontime next day the temperature had jumped thirty degrees.

That writer was rebelling shamefully against the Canadian winter. It was his moment of weakness. I had had mine that night in Winnipeg. In the weak moment we had in our imagination to hurl ourselves out of the Canadian experience, out and reject forever that myth growing in the country, pushed by some painters and poets who have gone into the Arctic, that the Canadian psyche has a subconscious awareness of the vast Arctic ice pack, the tremendous lonely frozen distances at the top of the country. This masked awareness is supposed to shape all our moods, our whole view of life. Being a city man who never was above the Arctic circle this romantic myth always struck me as utter eyewash.

I have only had a fugitive glimpse of that endless, frozen, silent land glistening in the sun, a glimpse from as far away as a hundred miles north of Edmonton. I was with a friend who knew a man who had some kind of a station for trappers. We drove in a car. The station manager and his Indian helper met us. They had a sleigh pulled by six huskies. That day there was a lot of sunlight. I stood looking north at the unbroken sweep of snow reaching to the horizon. You could say it had a kind of beauty, yes, but it was the beauty of a desert-if deserts have beauty in changing light-and it was monotonous. The Indian now was attending to the dogs. The manager asked me how I would like to go for a ride on the sled, driving the dogs myself. "Okay," I said. He gave me the two words for go and stop and showed me how to handle the reins. It was like driving a team of horses. I drove across the snow, all by myself, saying, "Mush, mush," and wondering how they would catch up to me if the dogs wouldn't turn back. But the dogs did turn, and my friends, watching me, were having a good laugh. Finally the Indian touched his head, he kept touching it as he grinned. At that time I was seeing many political dignitaries and I had been told that in Ottawa I would not be taken into the confidence of such men unless I wore a black homburg hat and a dark double-breasted overcoat, and there I was now on the dog sleigh, crying "Mush, mush," to the huskies in my black homburg and city coat. How, then, could I ever believe that I was secretly a creature of the Arctic ice pack. What a comic notion. When I left that vast desert of sunlit snow I knew I could never be one with it. I knew I could never believe that an awareness of this snow silence and the infinitude of pure white space lay buried in my soul as a shining bowl of pure white light: no!

How much closer to a man's moods and his longing for mystery is the feeling that comes watching the winter change, the entry into that other winter. It quickens the imagination. On the way to the west coast, whether you go by train, winding and circling through passes, or by planes that often circle around peaks just as endlessly, held up by snow storms ahead, the Rockies are never enchanting. They are too big, too hard, too grimly threatening in their savage winter hostility. But when you are through these giant gorges and towering peaks, coming into the British Columbia foothills, there is a magical transformation not only in the weather, but in a man's spirit too. Though it may be the end of February these hills are turning green, mists float in the deep valleys. You can believe that trolls and strange animals and friendly spirits are there. When you come into Vancouver you can throw off your winter coat. Crocuses are blooming, the bay looks blue and friendly. The mountain, the sleeping beauty, is in a soft haze. All this too is a part of the Canadian winter.

Ontario

Cape Breton, Nova Scotia

In a Vancouver hotel one February night, a middle-aged man, who had left the prairies to settle in Vancouver, started talking to me. He looked old for his age. Wiry and healthy, but old! "Yes, I miss the prairies." he said. "But let's face it. I was born in this country and in February too, and now I know I've had enough of the winter. No more prairie winters for me. Last year I said to myself, "I really don't have to put up with this anymore. So here I am. I like it here." But next day it was raining. For three days it rained, it was this damp heavy air that made me feel inert, I knew. Some clean bright snow would have been a relief; and that night I found myself thinking of an elderly doctor friend who had retired two years ago to California. He had sold everything; house, books, the old Ontario pine furniture – everything, and for two years had basked in the California sunlight. But two months ago I had met him, he was back in Toronto-to stay. The things he had missed you simply wouldn't believe, he said with an odd smile. Driving his car in the winter, for one thing. He had a special skill with it on ice. And rocking the car out of a deep snow rut; you use the gears, never racing the engine, you rock back and forth, back and forth in a gentle easy seductive motion and just roll out.

I was at my window now in my city home with my big white pup who had never known a snowy night. The snow had been falling for hours. It was nearly midnight. No one passing on the street had broken a path. I had to take the dog out so I went looking for the galoshes I hadn't used since last winter. Bundled up, I stepped out, the big young dog moving just as gingerly as I do in the deep snow. Then the pup began thrusting his nose in the snow, turning sometimes to look at me. Suddenly he started a slow leaping gallop, then, just as suddenly, whirled around, hurling himself forward fifty paces, then whirling back and leaping in the air as if he had found some magic in the snow that had to be celebrated in this wild ritual dance. Well, dogs and children love the snow, I thought. It wasn't cold out, there was no wind, and as I looked around I could remember very poignantly other city nights after a heavy snow fall with a little leap of satisfaction. It was not the satisfaction that the hunter, the skier, the snowmobiler, the skater, all those who go hurrying out to the countryside for their winter pleasures feel at the time of the first heavy snow. No, it was an awareness of the loveliness of the city in the snow, when the night is mild as it was now, and how I have liked being on the streets late at night after a heavy snowfall when the city has a white mask that hides the daytime ugly scars, and when the moon coming out suddenly touches with its winter light all the snow-covered roofs and spires and hardly anyone else is on the street. You can keep on walking for hours, feeling quiet quickening within you. It was on such a night, I remember it so brightly now, when I walked with a girl who had taken millinery lessons so she could design her own hats, and she had made this Chinese-looking hat, triangular strips of pink and black silk. We walked for hours in the city streets, not noticing that it had begun to snow again, and talked about going to Europe. When we finally went into a restaurant the new hat had turned into a bowl full of snow. It was ruined. But it didn't matter. The night had been given some kind of haunting beauty by the snow, a beauty that touched us, and I know this beauty is often felt by others in cities from Montreal to Regina. And, come to think of it, that old man I used to watch when I was a boy, the man who came out late at night and shovelled his neighbors' sidewalks, that man who bewildered us all, maybe in his own way he had been touched by this mild night city snow magic, as my dog was now, rollicking wildly on the corner under the street light.

New Brunswick

Magdalen Islands, Quebec

Igloolik, Northwest Territories

Ottawa River, Ontario

Quebec

Near Barrie, Ontario

Burgeo, Newfoundland

Maddox Cove, Newfoundland

Montreal, Quebec

Quebec

Prince Edward Island

Ontario

Prince Edward Island

British Columbia

New Brunswick

Igloolik, Northwest Territories

Ontario

Stanley Park, Vancouver, British Columbia

Burgeo, Newfoundland

Saskatchewan

Saint John River, New Brunswick

Prince Edward Island

Madawaska River, New Brunswick

Saskatchewan

Toronto, Ontario

Prince Edward Island

Fort McPherson, Northwest Territories

Barrie, Ontario

Ontario

Whitehorse, Yukon

Gulf of St. Lawrence

British Columbia

Near Banff, Alberta

British Columbia

Quebec

Near Halifax, Nova Scotia

Gulf of St. Lawrence

St. John's, Newfoundland

The Laurentians, Quebec

The Rockies

Northern Saskatchewan

Prince Edward Island

Burgeo, Newfoundland

Burgeo, Newfoundland

Simcoe County, Ontario

Manitoba

Ontario

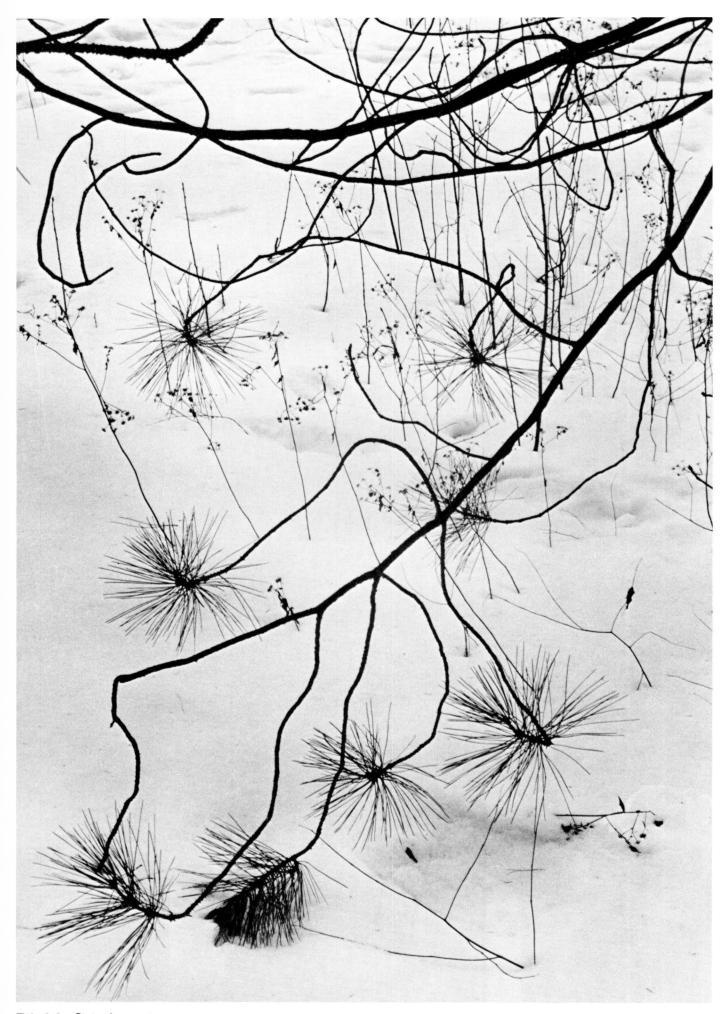

Erindale, Ontario

Upper Canada Village, Ontario

Trans-Canada Highway, Saskatchewan

The Laurentians, Quebec

Ontario

Grand Bruit, Newfoundland

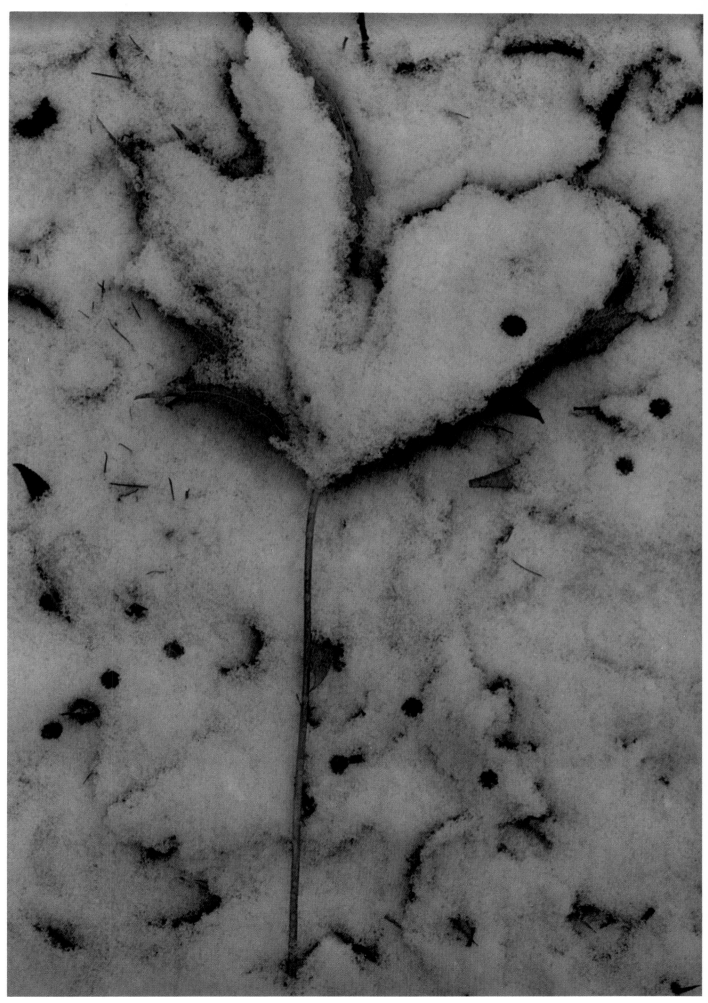

Toronto, Ontario

New Brunswick

Pond Inlet, Northwest Territories

Fraser River, British Columbia

Quebec

Grise Fjord, Ellesmere Island, Northwest Territories

Burgeo, Newfoundland

Manitoba

Banff, Bow River, Alberta

New Brunswick

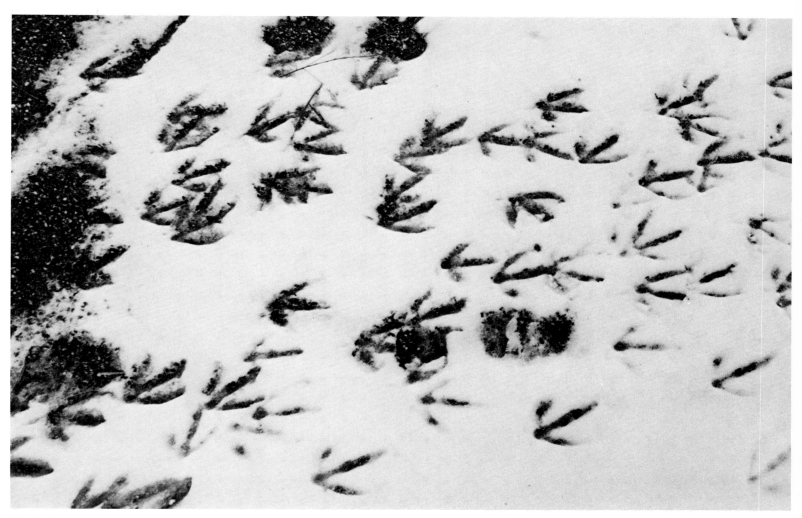

Manitoba

Labrador Sea

New Brunswick

Centre Island, Toronto, Ontario

Queen Charlotte Islands, British Columbia

Newfoundland

Quebec

Ontario

British Columbia

Upper Canada Village, Ontario

Magdalen Islands, Quebec

Vancouver, British Columbia

Saskatchewan

Banff-Jasper Highway, Alberta

Near Roberval, Quebec

South-west coast, Newfoundland

Notre Dame du Portage, Quebec

Morley Callaghan

Morley Callaghan was born in Toronto in 1903, graduated from St. Michael's College, studied law at Osgoode Hall, and was called to the Bar in 1928-the year in which his first novel, *Strange Fugitive,* was published in the United States. By that time he was already established as a writer of short stories and it was these, more than his novels, that gained him an international reputation. It was on their merits that Ernest Hemingway had had Callaghan printed in the Paris magazines and that F. Scott Fitzgerald recommended Callaghan to Scribner's.

Morley Callaghan is the author of three short story collections-*A Native Argosy, Now That April's Here* and *Morley Callaghan's Stories*-and a novella, *No Man's Meat.* His novels have included *It's Never Over, Broken Journey, Such Is My Beloved, They Shall Inherit the Earth, More Joy in Heaven, The Varsity Story, Luke Baldwin's Vow, The Loved and the Lost* (1951 Governor General's Award), *The Many Coloured Coat* and *A Passion in Rome.* His two plays-*Turn Home Again* and *Just Ask for George*-were produced in Toronto under the titles *Going Home* and *To Tell the Truth.* Memories of his years in Paris with Hemingway, Fitzgerald, Joyce and other great writers of that generation are contained in *That Summer in Paris.* Portions of a novel in progress, *The Dark and the Light of Lisa,* have recently been published.

John de Visser

John de Visser was born on February 8, 1930, in Veghel, The Netherlands, "a small town in rural Holland, not far from where both Pieter Breughal and Vincent Van Gogh spent their youths." In 1954 he took up photography and by 1957-58 had achieved his first publications, two large photo-essays on Toronto in *Maclean's*. He has since become established as one of Canada's best known and most respected photographers, recipient of the National Film Board Gold Medal and the Art Director's Show Award among others, contributor to more than fifty books and to major magazines throughout the world. He has collaborated on books, *This Rock Within the Sea* (with Farley Mowat) and *Heritage: A Romantic Look at Early Canadian Furniture* (with Scott Symons).

The photographic work of John de Visser has been called brilliant and revealing, beautiful and powerful. One reviewer has said that "de Visser does not take photographs-he paints the elements of life with a camera." Another has said, "de Visser is that rare genius to whom the lens becomes an instrument of inner vision."

A member of the Arts and Letters Club and the Royal Academy, de Visser has covered all of Canada in his work as a photographer, as well as travelling in that capacity to many parts of the world–Holland, Germany, Belgium, France, Spain, Italy, Switzerland, Austria, India, Russia and Siberia, the latter with Farley Mowat in 1969 and Prime Minister Pierre Trudeau in 1971. John de Visser considers Toronto his home.